Through The Ice On The Window

Emma Rutherford

BookLeaf Publishing

Presentation by *BookLeaf Publishing*

Web: www.bookleafpub.com

E-mail: info@bookleafpub.com

ISBN: 978-93-95088-14-5

First edition 2022

I dedicate these poems to my beloved son,
Nikolai.

ACKNOWLEDGEMENT

Thank you to everyone who loves me, hard as
that is a lot of the time.

PREFACE

Thank you to anyone who happens to read this.

Oxford Summer School

Campus in bed
Where are my headphones?
Tired and sore head....
First bus to Heathrow

Costa for breakfast
Welcome Club after check-in
I hate these chinos
Oh, how I miss this

Working and laughing and leaning on each
other's shoulders....
I forgot my jacket,
No worries, Russia's much colder.
I get back at eleven, up and ready for seven, I
feel older.
Still I'm dancing down the street.

If you're looking
If you're looking
For the job of your dreams
Go work for SBC
Go work for SBC.

Laughing and working with arms around each
other's shoulders,
I put on my jacket

I'm all packed and just like that, it's over.
9 hour bus ride home,
A year's wait is too long
I'm crying now, I told you,
How I miss you already.

If you're looking, if you're looking
For the job of your dreams,
Go work for SBC
Go work for SBC

The Glasses

The green light shows that the coffee stand's
open
We're playing in the park at the lake and I'm
hoping,
Luba comes along to give my son a ride on her
bike

Anna's got Timmy going down the slide
My son's chased a pack of pigeons into the sky
I'm riding the wave of this winter air's high

I've walked this lake round the turn of the
seasons; joy and pain, sun or rain, when I've
been searching for a reason.
I wish my footprints could stay marked in the
ground.

They call this place 'The Glasses'
That's what it looks like from above.
Yeah, they call this place 'The Glasses.'
This is a place I love.

Svobody Street

Butter yellow
Pastel blue
Buildings on each side
One long path leading through

From the bottom of Svobody Street
To the station at the end of the town
Past the fountain in the square
Going either up or down
I'd be happy either way
As long as we could meet

My Secret

Sun down
Wrong side of town
The bridge is well and truly up

It's too late
A taxi's not cheap
Any excuse to stay around.

Wine and cheese at your kitchen table
We'll watch Yes Minister and talk for as long as
we're able
Then blow out the candles and fall asleep on
your couch

You're my secret
Just not one that I can keep
You're my secret
Just not one that I can keep

Morning

It looks different now.
Your eyelids unstick
And a smile lights up your face,
I put some quiet jazz on
And we're ready for the day

Head through to the kitchen
I make breakfast while you play
We eat, you talk and fidget,
In the glow of the day
For the first time in a long time
Things are going my way

And I hope that's how they'll stay
And I hope that's how they'll stay.

Travel

Our French lecturer once told us that travel isn't
really travel anymore.
We take phones, tablets, laptops
So we're never really gone

Whilst I think there is a deep sadness in this; the
true peace of which we must feel bereft, it's
something for which I also long: the feeling of
being needed when I left.

The loneliest I ever felt was sitting on the night
train back to Moscow
You saw me to my seat and went back out
through the station concourse
It was 5:20am in the morning and everyone
around me was asleep
They at least could be blissfully unaware and
wake up where they needed to be

But all I could think of, as I sat there in the pitch
dark
My time up at home, my time there not yet
begun
Was all the lives being lived without me
As I travelled from point A-B
There is no one I can call right now
No one needs me at all

You Asked Me

You asked me, 'Does it touch you not, my friend?' It did. It does. More than you know. More than anyone can know. But, bound as we are by your dreams and my rules, it's not something I can ever let show.

Silence

It's never absolute; at least that's what I find
The hum of a fridge, the ping of a phone, the
buzzing of neon lights

And yet

For something that, by its very nature, should
indicate absence
I'm finding my silences far too full of late
The row may be over but the anger's thick
presence
Chokes the whole room out of air

At night I fill my head with other people's voices
To stop me pondering all my mistakes and bad
choices

Clueless

When you were 9 hours old, I had no idea how to parent you. I wasn't allowed to because you were an emergency C-section but that's a story for the 1 year post. 'Ah, well,' I thought, 'When he's 9 weeks, we'll be into a routine and I'll know what I'm doing.' And we were. But, at 9 weeks, you started sleeping through feeds and only nursing for a minute or two at a time. They told me my breasts weren't making enough milk so you were tiring yourself with the effort of nursing. They told me there must be something wrong with the bottles I was supplementing you with. They told me it must be something I ate. They told me my breasts must be infected or dirty.
"Ah, well," I thought, "When he's 9 months old, he'll be fully on bottles and solids." And you are. Except during the night. And I worry about you choking. Plus now you're crawling and wanting to touch everything. And they tell me it's about time you were walking. They tell me not to feed you the recipes I found and made for you.
"Ah, well," I think, "When you're 9 years old, you'll be at school and sleeping through the

night and eating safely." But what about mean classmates or teachers and homework?
In short, I am and always will be clueless when it comes to parenting you. But, when the effort of fighting them gets too much, I can always assure myself that by putting these expressions on your face, I must have some sort of clue!

Four Months Old

Your little hands have gone from screwed up
fists to completely open: may they always be
open to help and shake hands with all kinds of
people.
Your little eyes dart around taking everything in:
may you one day find a special someone to love
and look into their eyes forever.
No matter how straight on I lie you down in
your cot, you always manage to shift into an
angle: may you never be afraid to stop moving
until you find a place you want to stay.
You keep trying to pick up your toys with your
mouth: may you never lose that inventive and
creative spirit.
I love you Nikolai Antonovich Volkov.

The Letter

We've grown up and on enough now
To look back and find it cute
That letter I wrote you at age 21
Confessing my love for you

You told me it's there in the attic
I'll bet now it's covered in dust
The paper's still there, the words still inscribed
But the meaning's like paint turned to rust

Transition

They say it's not good to transition too quickly
Like when you work out and your heart rate's
up; you shouldn't stop suddenly, but gradually
bring the heart rate down, rather than jam the
system with a shock

I like that idea of blood going from pumping to
flowing
Instead of waves smashing against the rocks of
my veins
It's more...a brook running over stones

In the same way, on the train that day
A feeling of inception
The scenery outside so single minded
Only forest trees in front and behind
The snow and ice that used to enchant
Hanging like crystals from every branch
Are now just an endless, muddy expanse

But I still wouldn't want to skip straight to the
sun
My heart's not ready for that quite yet
I've still got some digging and exploring to do
Things I can only find in the mud

Brokenness

It's sunrise at the entrance to the castle
I'm not quite sure how or why I got here
Or what the route back is
Or if I'm even meant to go back at all
And instead go forward and move.....where?
On?

I'm not complaining either way
Which is unusual for me
Normally, I'm scouting out the nearest cafe,
The closest place I can touch base

I go inside and the first room has a floor that's
covered in fractals of smokey quartz. I pick a
piece up and place it against my forehead; as I
pull it away I almost expect to see the wisps of
my negative thoughts stuck to it, having left me
for good.

Instead I see something else. Each shard is a
minute piece of a jigsaw puzzle. In one shard my
eye is creased from laughter, in the other, it's
almost permanently narrowed, against the wind,
against the snow, against the onslaught of my
thoughts. In the third, it's hollow and purple
shadows loom large.

I see now why I'm here; I'm supposed to put the
pieces of me back together.
But do I build a new one or improve on what
I've got?
I think I'll be here a while.......

A Coffee Bean

I wait with all the others as I stare at you
I'm not sure what's led you here or what you're
going through
Others like you, I know quite well
But you're new with your own story to tell

Whatever form you want me to take,
I'll do it to help you get through the day

Non-Movie Scene

If this were our very own movie scene,
We'd be standing on a bridge in some city at
night in the rain
All out of breath, emotions running high
Both in tears after some pointless fight.

'Do you love me?' you'd cry in despair.
'I don't know...I want to!' I'd wail.
'Well, that's not enough,' you'd say then, 'So
long!'
Then, as you turned to walk away,
I'd chase after you and get hit by a car.
You'd cradle me in your tender arms.
And, as I woke in the hospital,
To the movie's final song
We'd both realise what the audience knew all
along.

But this is a non-movie scene
We're on the phone but I can almost see
Your eyes screwed up as you pluck up the will
To ask me the question whose answer, still,
won't, can't, change anything.

'Do you love me? In that way?' There it is.
I know the answer I want to give, but I won't.

Because, if I said I loved you, it would be a
tragedy for us both.
Besides, I suspect, you already know.

The Storm

The way I remember it, there was the kind of
thunder storm
That's only fun when you're not alone.
The lightning flash lit up the room
Then thunder with a deafening boom

And it that moment I saw so clearly
Every object in the room around me.
I could almost feel them.

But this is a different kind of storm.
There's no way out that lightning can illuminate.
The thunder clouds still loom heavy
And the rain can fall all it wants
But the ground will still be parched.

Fast Food

It's nice to have some stability;
It definitely makes a change
She likes that each day looks exactly the same.

He comes in to have somewhere to go,
To get away from the silence of home.
He likes the fact that they know his order.
It makes him feel like he matters.

My New Home

25

He was packing up his flat and noticed me;
I was in the pile, out of luck, my next stop; the
rubbish truck.
I'd seen it coming for a while,
He no longer looked at me and smiled.

His colleague visited me one day,
So he asked 'Would your wee nephew like to
play with this old toy of mine?'
He got here in the nick of time!

He said, 'Yes' and now my new home
Is with a little boy all my own
Who will love me until he's grown.
And his mum will make sure I'm passed along,
to his small daughter or son.

Voices In The Wires

I once watched a nature program that described
how trees talk to each other by sending
electronic signals through the ground.

And how the old trees, even as they die, send out
the last of their energy through these same
signals; so the young ones can have the best
chance in life.

As below, so above?
Do these same trees, which have the telephone
wires tangled through their leaves, hear our
voices in the wires?
The sighs, cries, pleas and stammers?
I pity them, that they have to hear all that.

And yet, I envy them.
We don't yet know the words to keep ourselves
truly alive.

And we've lost the voices of our ancestors; ones
I fear we'll never reclaim.

The Other Me

No one covered me with a blanket that day, so I
covered myself.
My body had gone into fight or flight and all I
could see, hear, taste, feel was white.
As I lay in a foetal position on the bed, I made
sure to close my eyes and see.....

The other me.

The one in the white cotton t-shirt and pink
pinafore with the clunky black lace-up shoes.
She's cycling along a river. She's writing in a
cafe. She doesn't mind taking those photos of her
happy, couple friends holding hands as they
walk away.

She's patient with herself. She waits and trusts.
She listened to God that night on the river when
He said, 'I have so much more for you than this.'

The Tower Guard

I've always thought it distinctly odd
That we house patients right at the top
Of the hospital grounds
It's as though they have no place left to go in the
world
So why not place them in the waiting room
On the hill below the clouds?

My fellow guard tells me I'm a fool;
That what we are doing is neither unusual nor
cruel:
'After all, if you were them, what would you
rather do? Look down on the city or have them
look down on you?'

I look down on them but in the literal sense,
From my guard tower which overlooks the
boundary fence.
I see them work the garden every day
Like children let out of school to play.

One of them always glances up my way
Over his shoulder and waves
I don't respond, or return his wave
I'm not allowed to know his name

But I still wasn't ready for that day
He tried to make a getaway
I fired my dart and brought him down
As everyone crowded round

I'll never be sure, but I could swear
I'll remember till my dying day
How, as the light started to fade
He tried to look at me and wave.

www.ingramcontent.com/pod-product-compliance
Lightning Source LLC
Chambersburg PA
CBHW060923130726

48001CB00006B/2376